# *Roblox*
# *How To Draw*
## Cute Animacule

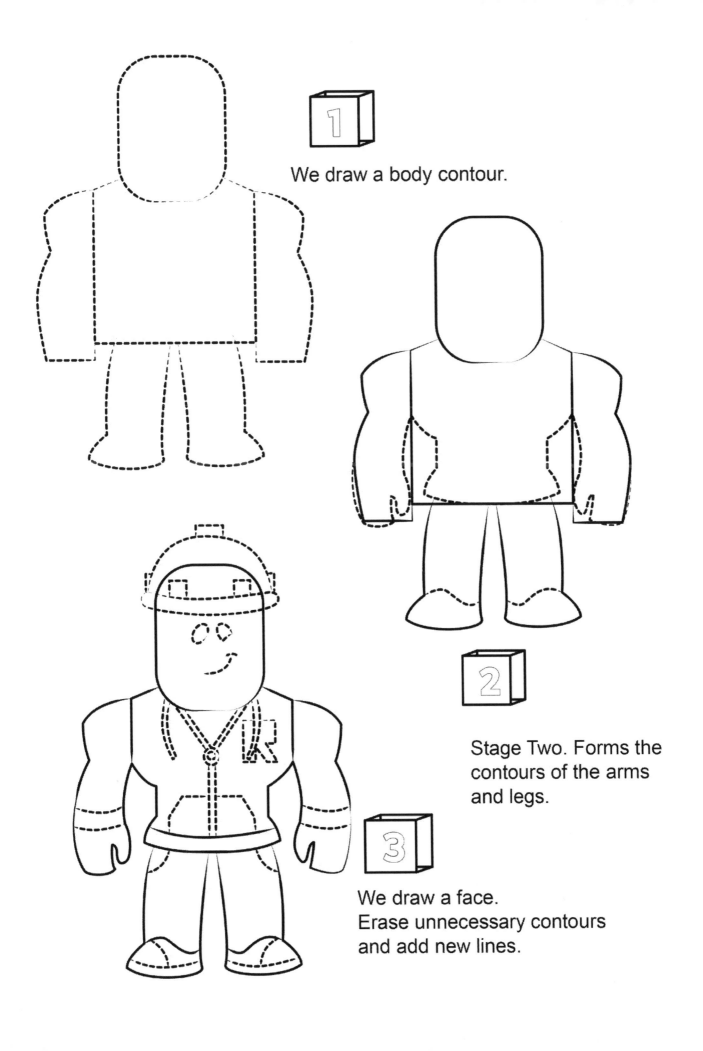

We draw a body contour.

Stage Two. Forms the
contours of the arms
and legs.

We draw a face.
Erase unnecessary contours
and add new lines.

# Practice Page

ROBLOX

4

We remove all unnecessary
elements and color
the final version.

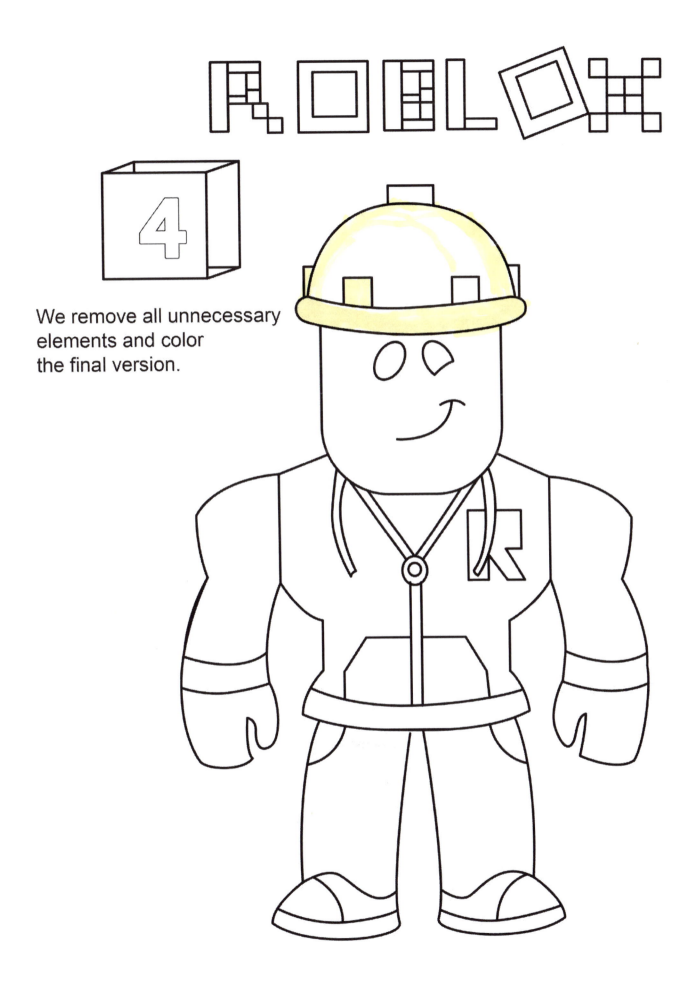

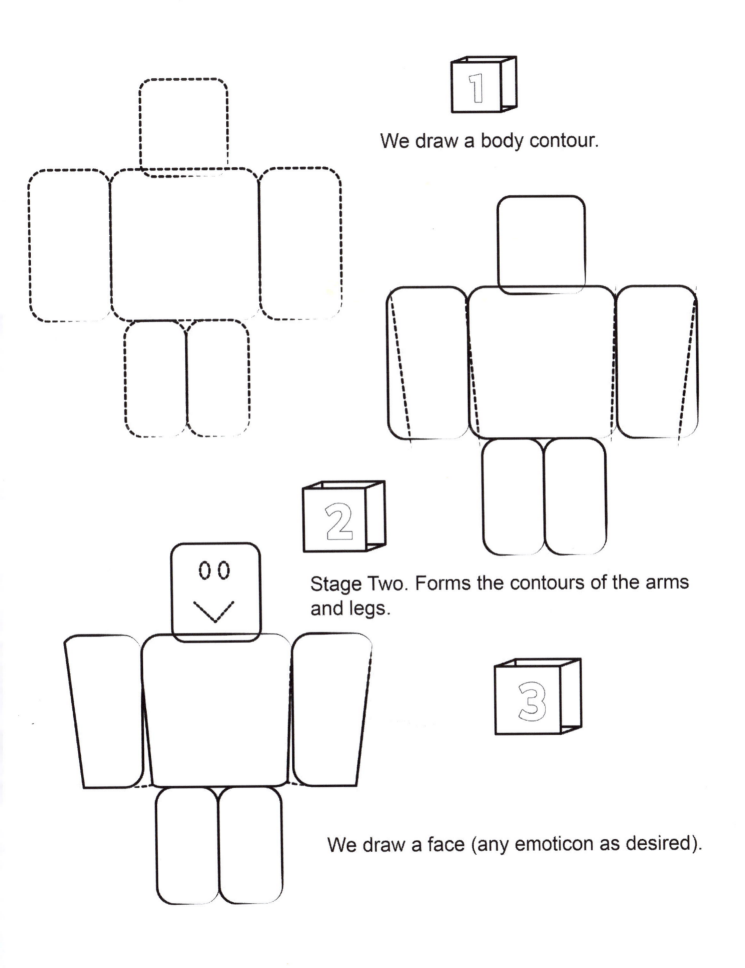

We draw a body contour.

Stage Two. Forms the contours of the arms and legs.

We draw a face (any emoticon as desired).

# Practice Page

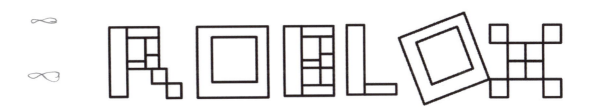

The final stage. We draw our figure and color it.

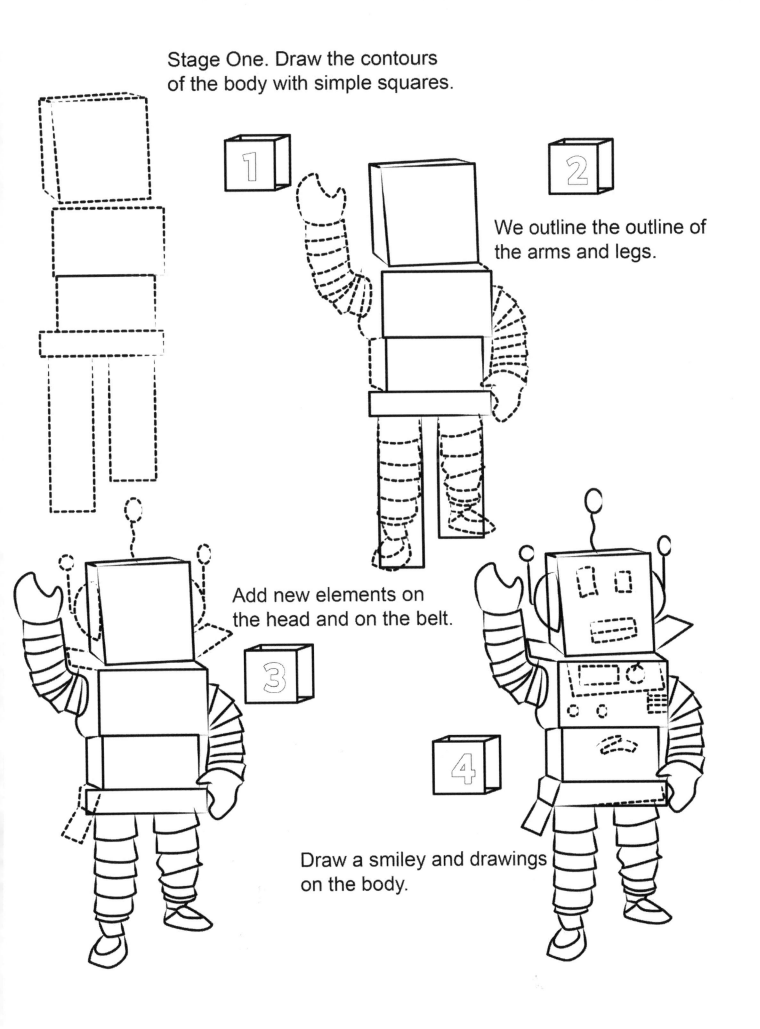

Stage One. Draw the contours of the body with simple squares.

1

2

We outline the outline of the arms and legs.

Add new elements on the head and on the belt.

3

4

Draw a smiley and drawings on the body.

# Practice Page

The final stage. We erase all
unnecessary lines and color as desired.

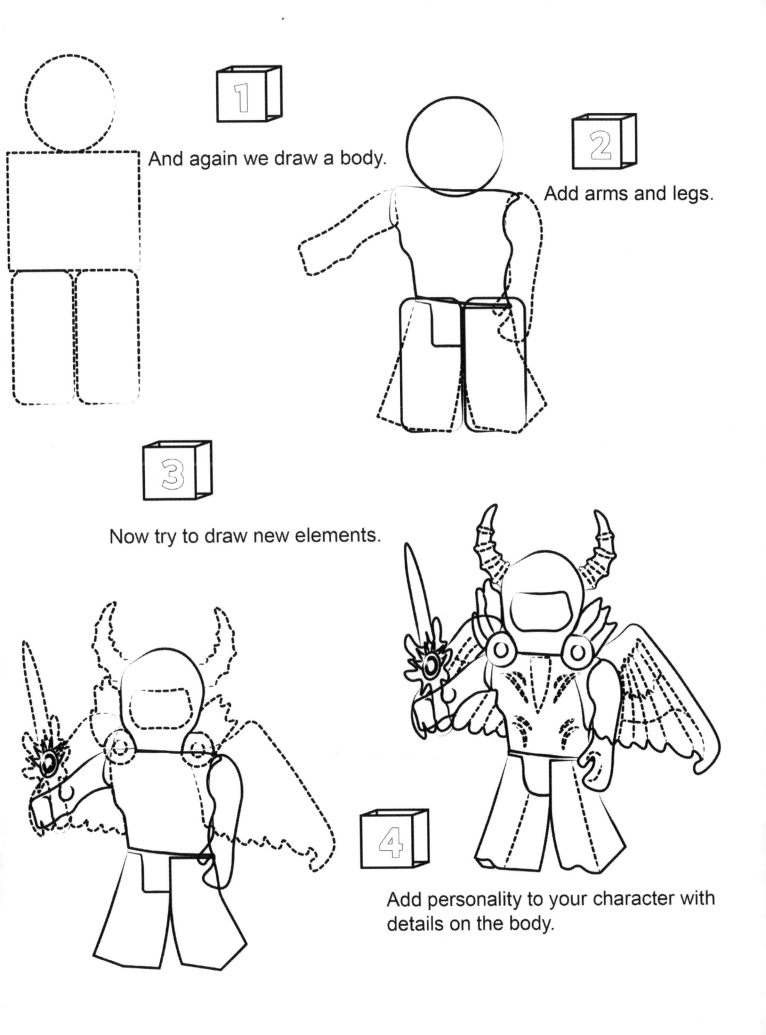

And again we draw a body.

Add arms and legs.

Now try to draw new elements.

Add personality to your character with details on the body.

# Practice Page

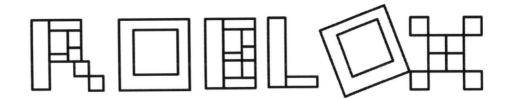

Cut off unnecessary lines and color.

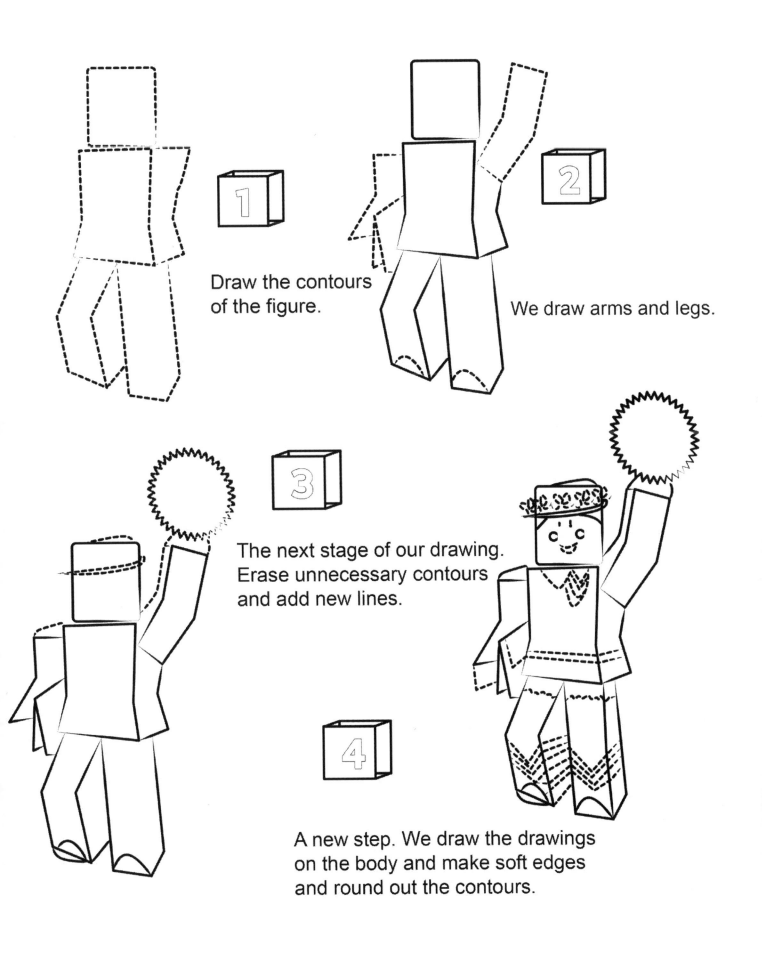

Draw the contours
of the figure.

We draw arms and legs.

The next stage of our drawing.
Erase unnecessary contours
and add new lines.

A new step. We draw the drawings
on the body and make soft edges
and round out the contours.

# Practice Page

Do not forget to erase excess lines.
Add any drawings to the body
and color your character.

**1** First stage. Simple body shapes.

We need arms and legs. Let's draw them. **2**

**3** Now we make him hair. Making a broom in the hand.

**4** Add face and hair. We make the figure more beautiful.

# Practice Page

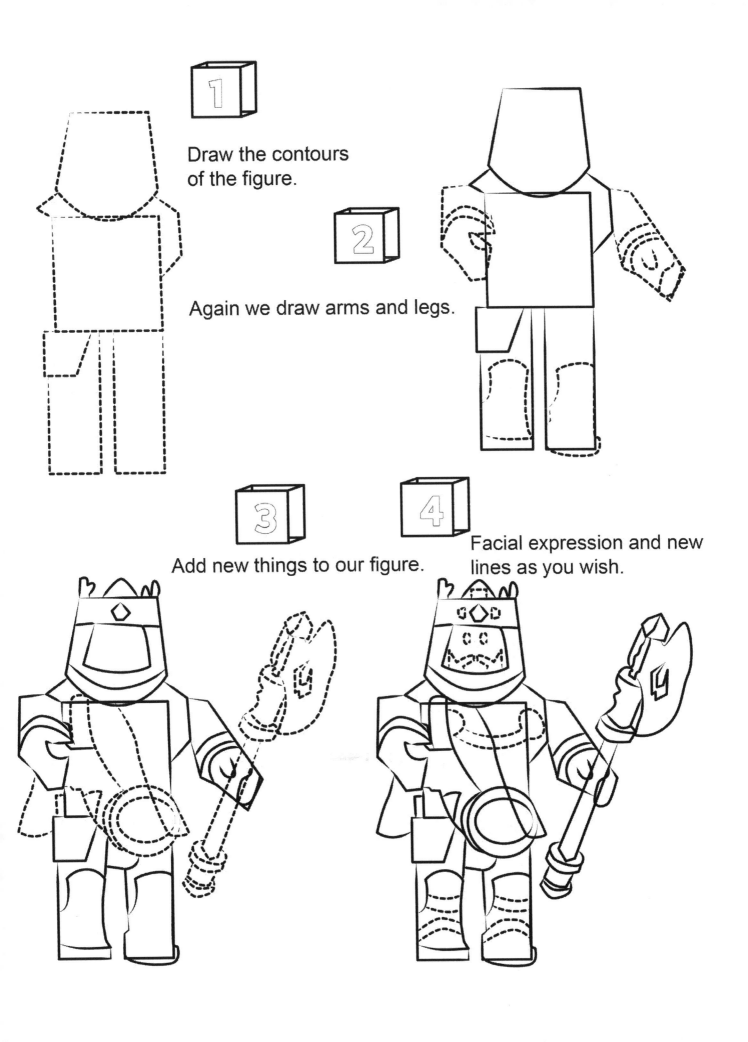

Draw the contours of the figure.

Again we draw arms and legs.

Add new things to our figure.

Facial expression and new lines as you wish.

# Practice Page

We erase the unnecessary and colorize.

**1** Draw the contours of the figure.

**2** We draw arms and legs.

**3** The next stage of our drawing. Erase unnecessary contours and add new lines.

**4** A new step. We draw the drawings on the body.

# Practice Page

We remove all unnecessary elements
and color the final version.

Draw the contours of the figure.

We make arms and legs.

Erase unnecessary lines and add pictures on the body.

We draw a gun and a hairstyle.

# Practice Page

Practice Page

Final stage. We draw an interesting mask on the face and color it.

And again we draw a contour.

We form arms and legs.

It's time for the dragon,
make him funny and cute.
And add points to the hero.

Edit the shape as desired
and add new lines.

# Practice Page

It's time to colorize everything.

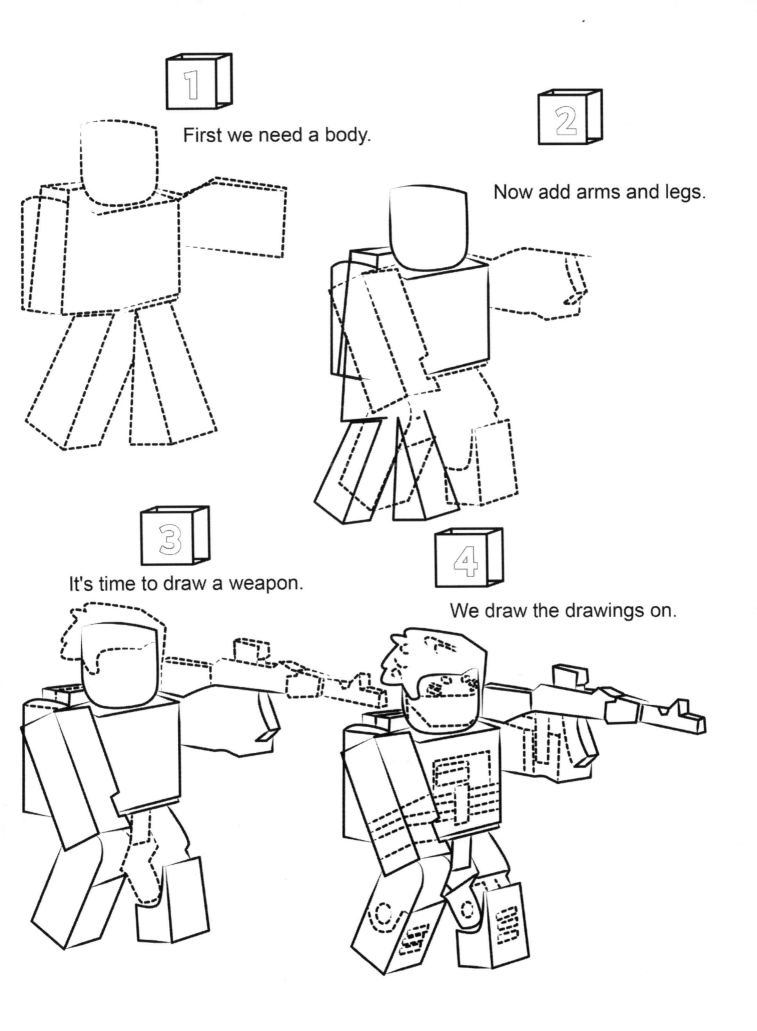

# Practice Page

We remove all unnecessary elements
and color the final version.

**1** Draw the contours of the figure.

**2** We draw arms and legs.

**3** The next stage of our drawing. Erase unnecessary contours and add new lines.

**4** A new step. We draw the drawings on the body and make soft edges and round out the contours.

# Practice Page

Do not forget to erase excess lines.
Add any drawings to the body
and color your character.

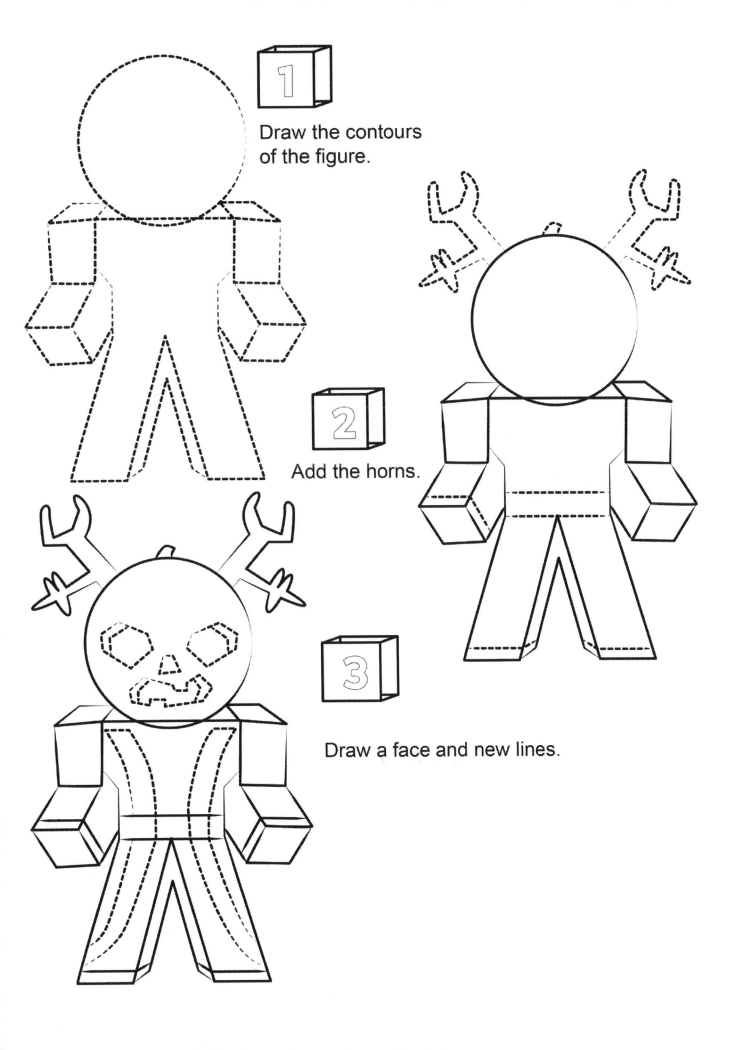

1 Draw the contours of the figure.

2 Add the horns.

3 Draw a face and new lines.

# Practice Page

We remove all unnecessary elements and color the final version.

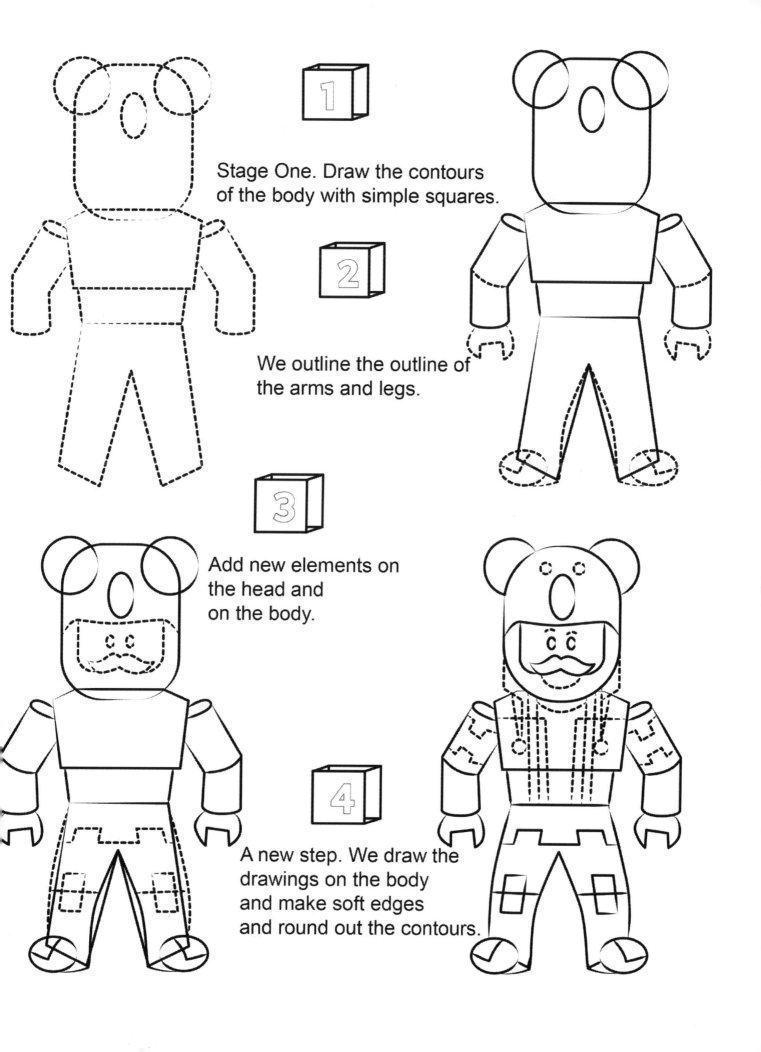

Stage One. Draw the contours of the body with simple squares.

We outline the outline of the arms and legs.

Add new elements on the head and on the body.

A new step. We draw the drawings on the body and make soft edges and round out the contours.

# Practice Page

# ROBLOX

**5** Paint your hero.

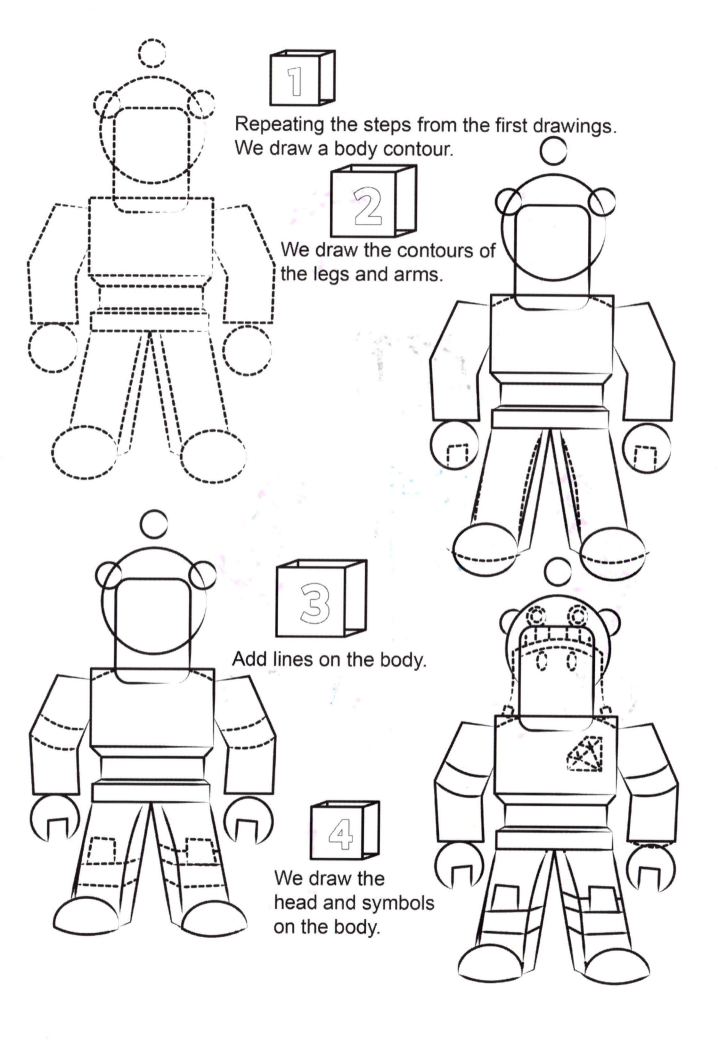

**1** Repeating the steps from the first drawings. We draw a body contour.

**2** We draw the contours of the legs and arms.

**3** Add lines on the body.

**4** We draw the head and symbols on the body.

# Practice Page

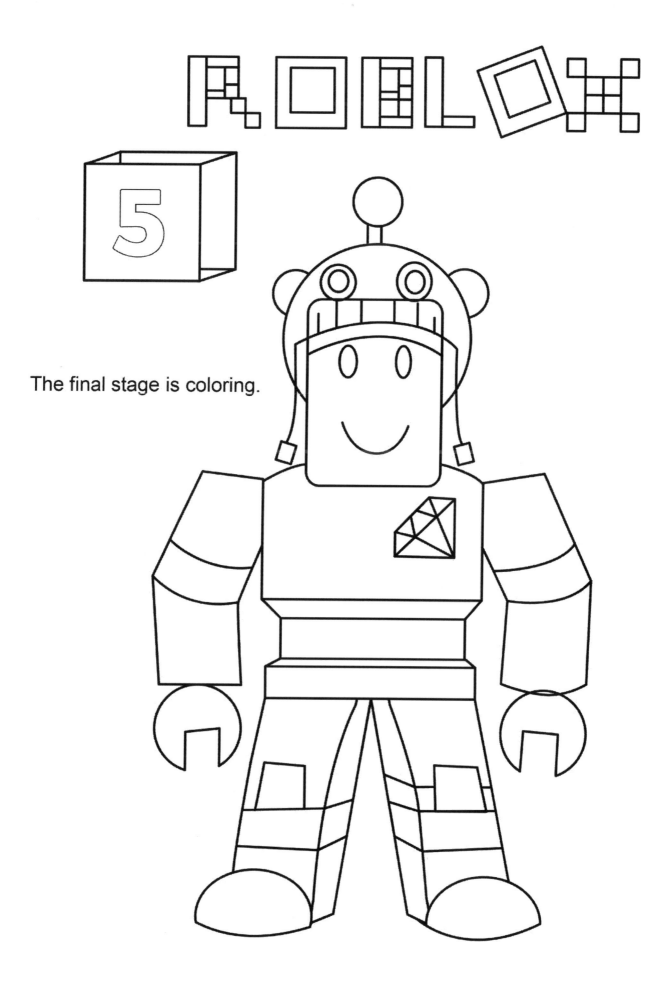

The final stage is coloring.

Repeating the steps from the first drawings. We draw a body contour.

Improving legs and arms.

Learning to draw pigtails.

Add the face and drawings on the body.

# Practice Page

5

Coloring our figure. If you want,
add small elements on the body.

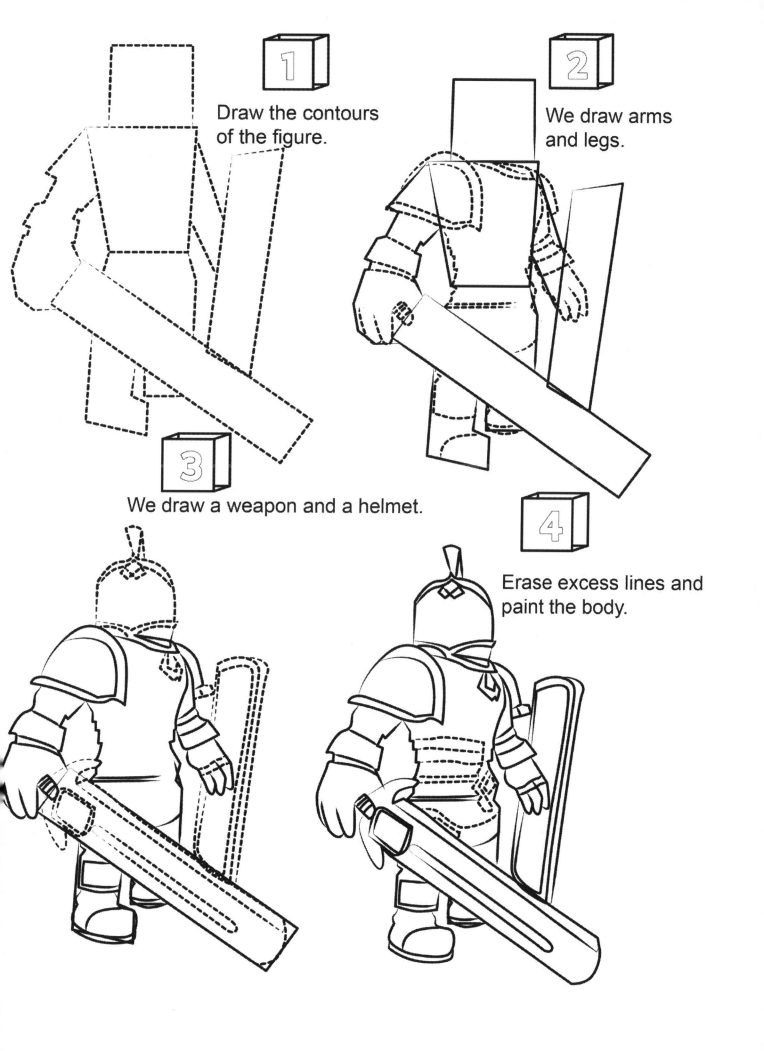

**1** Draw the contours of the figure.

**2** We draw arms and legs.

**3** We draw a weapon and a helmet.

**4** Erase excess lines and paint the body.

# Practice Page

ROBLOX

5

It's time to colorize everything.

**1** First stage. Simple body shapes.

**2** We need arms and legs. Let's draw them.

**4** We draw a face and drawings on the body.

**3** We make the contours more rounded. And add weapons.

# Practice Page

ROBLOX

5

Do not forget to erase excess lines.
Add any drawings to the body
and color your character.

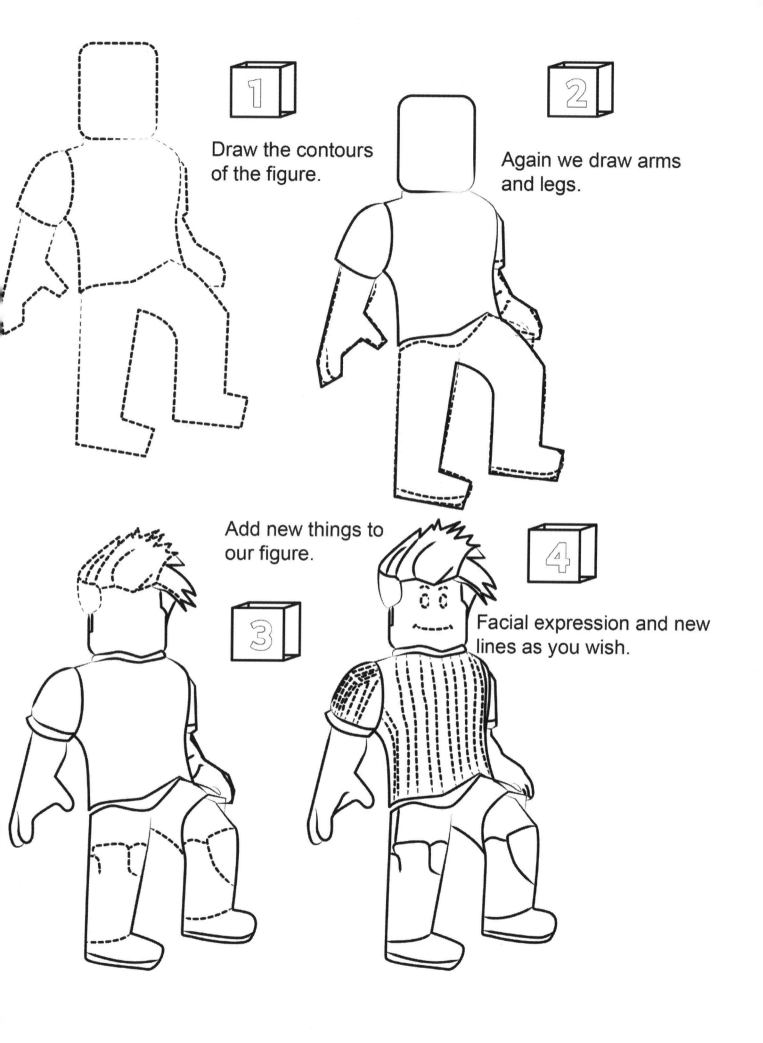

**1** Draw the contours of the figure.

**2** Again we draw arms and legs.

Add new things to our figure. **3**

**4** Facial expression and new lines as you wish.

# Practice Page

ROBLOX

5

We erase the unnecessary
and colorize.

1 Draw the contours of the figure.

2 We draw the contours of the arms and legs.

3 Add new elements for the character.

4 Next stage. We make a face and a body.

# Practice Page

We remove all unnecessary elements and color the final version.

1 Draw the contours of the figure.

2 We make arms and legs.

3 We draw a sword, hair and wings.

4 Erase unnecessary lines and add pictures on the body.

# Practice Page

Practice Page

ROBLOX

Final stage. Color it.

And again we draw a contour.

We form arms and legs.

Add new items.

Draw the satchel on the back and remove the unnecessary lines.

# Practice Page

We draw a face. Color
the final version.

Draw the contours of the figure.

Now add arms and legs.

It's time to draw a weapon.

We draw the drawings on.

# Practice Page

We remove all unnecessary
elements and color the final version.

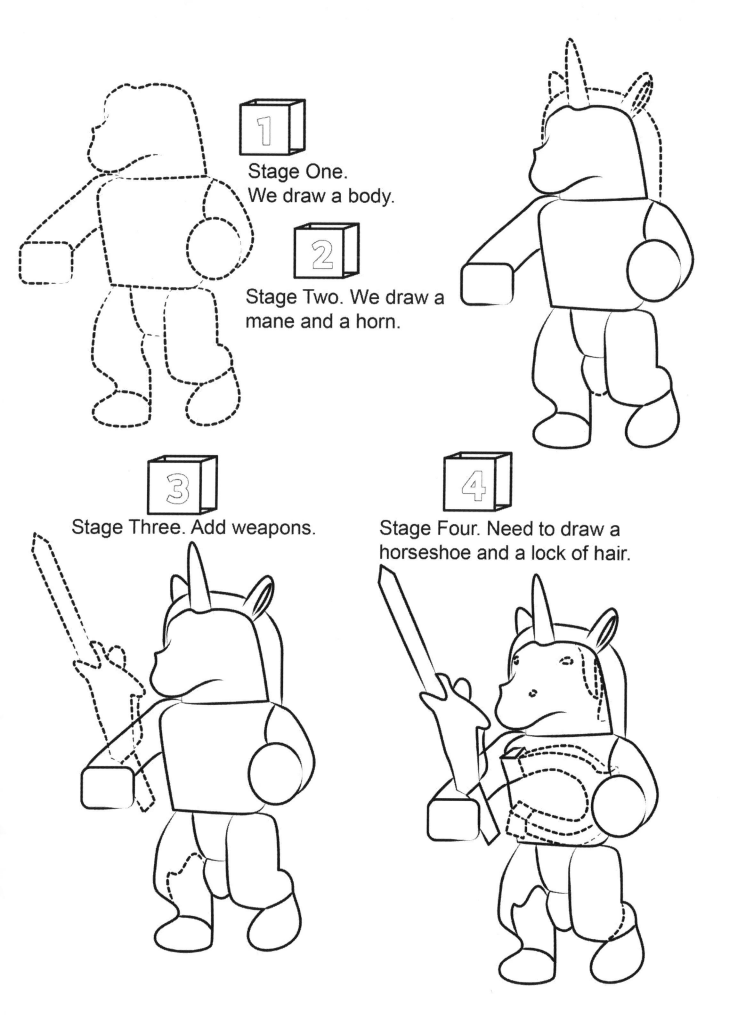

**Stage One.** We draw a body.

**Stage Two.** We draw a mane and a horn.

**Stage Three.** Add weapons.

**Stage Four.** Need to draw a horseshoe and a lock of hair.

# Practice Page

Final stage. All this needs to be colored.

And again we draw a body.

Add arms and legs.

Now try to draw new elements.

A new step. We draw the
drawings on the body
and make soft edges
and round out the contours.

# Practice Page

Coloring our figure.
If you want, add small
elements on the body.

Printed in Great Britain
by Amazon